THIS TIME

Gerald A. Brinsdon

Stourbridge

June 1988

OTHER COLLECTIONS OF POEMS BY RUTH FAINLIGHT:

Cages
Eighteen Poems from 1966
To See the Matter Clearly
Poems (with Ted Hughes and Alan Sillitoe)
The Region's Violence
Twenty-one Poems
Another Full Moon
Sibyls and Others
Climates
Fifteen to Infinity
Selected Poems
The Knot
Sibyls

THIS TIME OF YEAR

A COLLECTION OF POEMS

RUTH FAINLIGHT

SINCLAIR-STEVENSON

First published in Great Britain in 1993
by Sinclair-Stevenson
an imprint of Reed Consumer Books Ltd
Michelin House, 81 Fulham Road, London SW3 6RB
and Auckland, Melbourne, Singapore and Toronto

Reprinted 1994

ISBN: 1 85619 346 2

A CIP catalogue record for this book
is available from the British Library

Typeset by Rowland Phototypesetting Limited,
Bury St Edmunds, Suffolk

Printed and bound in Great Britain
by Cox & Wyman Ltd, Reading, Berks

ACKNOWLEDGEMENTS

The *Charleston Magazine*
Critical Quarterly
The Duncan Lawrie Journal
Jewish Quarterly
The *London Magazine*
London Review of Books
The *New Yorker*
The Observer
Poetry Book Society Anthology 2
Poetry Durham
PN Review
Poetry Review
Southwest Review
The *Spectator*
The *Threepenny Review*
Times Literary Supplement

'Twelve Sibyls' was first published with twelve woodcuts
by Leonard Baskin in a limited edition by The Gehenna
Press, USA.

CONTENTS

I
Mottoes   3
Out to Lunch   4
A Couple   5
Warped Toward the North   6
The Author   7
My Lucky Star   8
A Village Story   9
A Saga   12
Galatea   13
Phallic Sapphics   14
The Necklace   15
Romance   16
Homage   18
A Mourner   19
Lark   20
Until You Read It   21

II
This Time of Year   25
The Coptic Wedding   27
Lineage   29
Choosing   30
Nails and Spiders and Jacks   31
The X-Ray Machine   33
Clinging Ivy   34
Tosca   35

III
Bird and Worm   39
The Old Dog   40
The Fish   41
Visitation   42
Reflection   43
Part of the Crowd   44
Privacy on Lake Ohrid   45

The Law   47
To Whom It Pertains   48
The Plastic Bag   49
The Problem   50

IV
New-Born   55
The Cranes   58
Late Low Sun   59
Flowing Stream   61
Thunder   62
Buds   63
Solstice   64
On the Coast Road   65
Veronica's Napkin   66
Art   67
Chardin's 'Jar of Apricots'   68
Arshile Gorky's Mother   69

TWELVE SIBYLS
Squatting at the Womb's Mouth   73
Sibyl Hands   74
Facts About the Sibyl   75
After Possession   76
Profiles   77
His Face   78
Dreamy   79
Weighty   80
Inward   81
What Greater God . . .   82
Elegant Sibyl   83
The Egg Mother   84

I

MOTTOES

If you run with the hare
and hunt with the hounds
you fall between two stools.
No changing horses in mid-stream.
Where you make your bed
you have to lie,
among roses and thorns. Really,
it's like the boy who cried, 'Wolf!'
when he saw a lost dog from the pack.
In the land of the blind
the one-eyed man – so don't try,
we all know how it ends.

OUT TO LUNCH

Always on the look-out
for God's talent scout
(eyes sliding up and down and round)

Pushy and anxious
as an out-of-work actress
(imagining he might be Dracula)

Always on the look-out
for God's talent scout
(outright smile, worn-out teeth, outsize mouth)

Just sanguine enough
to out-class the others
(but ugh, love – not from the jugular!)

Always on the look-out
for God's talent scout
who's gone to ground

or somewhere out of town
with the Count.
(He's out of this world.)

A COUPLE

As smug as death,
Daphne and Dorian Gray,
eternal honeymooners,
plunge into another tango.

To be forever young
seemed the best gift
to ask of the Devil.
Since then, they must have danced
ten times around the world.

Like melting sugar skulls
at a Todos Santos picnic
in Mexico City,
or a gallant hussar's
fancy epaulettes,

those perched smiles
above each other's shoulder –
mimicking a lust that bores them.
Mais toujours la politesse.

WARPED TOWARD THE NORTH

Warped toward the North,
magnet pulsing at the polar core
with the hot glint and dull throb of a brazier

or a lit-up liner freighted
with wordless dancers, sequins swaying
on the hems of their skirts, and their tuxedoed partners

the moment before the boilers
burst and orchestra and sailors
plunged through fire and steam and frothing water.

The bald white brow of
a whale or a god, arms as soft
as snowdrifts, or Death's cradle, but strong enough

to save me from the devastation,
are attributes of my Angel.
His song so beautiful that I forget the South.

THE AUTHOR

I feel no need for what is called real
life – enough in my writing. (Which shows
such wisdom, warmth and worldly *nous*,
they say, one might easily think
I'd gone everywhere, done everything,
been a slave, an explorer, a diplomat,
even a tree or a bird or a horse.)

I stay at home each day, sit
at my desk most of the night, with no
desire for anyone except
the characters who move between
the page and my imagination.
There was a time I had to smile,
adapt, and learn it all, observe
the faces, attend the conversation.
But I've almost forgotten the hard facts.
Or I confuse them with the fictions.

There used to be friends. Now they don't seem
necessary. So much happened,
I could think about it forever.
I run the action through again
and listen to those voices from the past.
There is always something new
to alter. And my dreams get better.

MY LUCKY STAR

Just to imagine the smell of his quarters,
the state of his linen and wardrobe,
makes one nauseous (you were supposed
to love him, warts and all):
that arrogant and alcoholic
clerkish solipsistic charmer
who cannot manage to keep even
his manuscripts in order.

Always in the background (in spite of or
because of? an unresolved, almost
Pavlovian misogyny)
is that essential dual support-system:
a 'woman of the people' who sometimes
lets him fuck her, and the other,
upper-class, innocent whose stern
profile he worships from a distance.

The history of European culture
confirms the same pattern
from the Tagus to the Urals.
(I'm talking about the only model
of 'artist' on offer: those daunting groupie-
hagiographies I read, as a girl.)
But I recovered, apostate:
thank my lucky star.

A VILLAGE STORY

Under the canopy of plane trees
shading the plaza in full summer,
young girls of the village,
    the butterfly sleeves and wide stiff skirts
    of their starched cotton dresses
    (pink, blue, green, white and yellow –
    pale virginal colours)
    speckled by disks of sunlight
    filtered through the branches,
are standing in small groups
with hands or arms linked together,
shocked into silence –
to watch an act of public penance.

        On her knees
        in the square
     near the fountain and church
       in front of the cafe
     the place where it happened.

The daughter-in-law, pallid and swollen-eyed,
serving drinks to the tourists,
looks stupid with shame,
like someone beaten half-conscious.
But those discoloured patches of skin on her face
are not bruises. She is pregnant.

Her husband moves between the bar
and the cafe's open door
as if treading water.
His head is in another element.
The body –
     'strong as a bull, tall as a fishing-boat's mast',
     covered with black hair
     that sprouts below the cuffs, curls above the neck,
     of a perfectly-pressed white shirt –
was the cause of the problem.
The expression on his small-featured face
is haughty, reproving, and frightened.
His eyes will not focus.
He has poured out the cognacs and coffees,
mixed the *horchatas*, so often
it has become automatic.

            In the square
         near the fountain and church
          in front of the cafe
   the sinner, the mother, the mother-in-law,
       the woman disgraced,
          on her knees
       making public repentance,

a deep-breasted vigorous matron
like a Mediterranean goddess
almost as tall, surely as strong, as her son.

Since the time of the troubles, the old man
has stayed on their farm in the hills
with his books and his guns.
His wife and son have always run the cafe –
where they, the other children
and the young wife, live upstairs.

Public repentance.
On her knees in the square.
Hands upraised and head thrown back,
glinting eyes and open mouth,
like every holy picture on the altar.
Doing what the priest told her

after the door was forced
the sheet torn off
the two of them caught
in her wide matrimonial bed,
where he might have been conceived,
and where he was born.

Whatever his penance, it was endured in private.
The couple brazened it out, dealing with tourists
in stoical silence. The others went somewhere else
for the rest of the season, as if into hiding.

That winter, once the grandchild had been born,
she came down from the farm
wearing black, a widow, prouder than ever.
The young girls could not stop watching and talking.
The young men adored her.

A SAGA

Cold scents the path.
Cold ores salt the caves and cliffs.
Stars sift light
through the black veil night wears,
and the sea nudges against the rocky breasts of earth.

On the weed-strewn beach
below the walls of the castle keep
she gathers bands of purple kelp
curled tight as a whip
and watches the horizon change:
Azure. Ultramarine. Indigo.

Beyond that line
where ocean plunges down the edge of the world
and the sky curdles and thickens and follows over,
each yearning to meet the other,
a high-prowed boat with russet sails is moving closer.

GALATEA

– woke from a statue's dream
on the night of full moon
(May's Milk-Moon)
her whole body altered:

with the moist gleam of marble
under quarry-dust,
flesh through talcum powder,
caked breasts stone-hard:

a spangled web of pores
patterning the skin
like an astronaut's map
or a fountain of stars.

PHALLIC SAPPHICS

Close your eyes against accordion angles
opening out like ivory fans, poker
hands and velvet theatre curtains, or bivalves
to the swirling tide.

Watch instead a runnel of lime-charged water
slowly drip from a stalactite to pattern
the slick wet sides and floor of a karstland cave
with mineral lace.

Remember the bird you once held on your palm,
how it struggled to fly? Its hot hard feathers
in panic-flutter were striped with the same pale
onyx colours as

shingle under almost invisible waves,
or smooth skin sliding through my practised fingers.
The bird was blinded by fear. Your eyes narrow
in expectation.

THE NECKLACE

Someone sent beads for a necklace,
an unexpected gift. When I
opened the bag of soft rubbed chamois
and loosed the knotted leather cord
they spilled across the floor like those
first rolling drops of rain
coated with summer dust that seem to be
quicksilver, or threshed grain poured.

They were jade, coral, amber,
streaky mineral and polished
metal, clear and clouded glass –
beads of every shape and sort.

I peered under the furniture,
crawled through the table legs, trying
to find them among the carpet's tufts
where they nestled like insect eggs.
I searched the hearthstone's ashy corners.
The shards of jetty coal and cinder
and splinters of carbonised wood might have
been beads. I think I got them all.

A man was there, who laughed as he watched.
But I can't tell you who he was
or what happened next. I didn't
thread that necklace in my dream.

ROMANCE

Every time I fold the laundry
I remember when she told me how
it took an hour to put his clothes away,
and that meant every day.

Eyes flashing, she made the list
of her duties into a metaphor.
She looked like a Minoan goddess, or Yeats'
princess bedded on straw.

She seemed to gloat on oppression,
as if it were the fuel and source
of her obsession, and each passionate protest
a further confirmation.

My spirit shrivelled, like fingers
from harsh soap and cold water,
to hear this version of the same old story.
Yet I could not doubt her.

Fairy-tales are very specific,
almost domestic – tasks to be done,
problems to solve. They tell about bewitched
princesses, toad princes,

and the force that holds them spell-bound.
Smoothing his shirts, she dreamed
of transformation and reward, and being
happy ever after.

I'd gone down that road before,
and knew its forks and sudden twists
where one false step has mortal consequence.
But I was luckier.

HOMAGE

It's not a case of forget or forgive.
Who expects either?
Something different happens.
I haven't forgotten
what you did to me or what I did.
I think about it often.
A steady contemplation
can dissolve the need for action,
as acid soil consumes bones, cloth, wood.
After a time, even the metal's gone.
Nor have I forgiven.
Forgiveness would be understanding
why those burials were so elaborate.
To the few surviving rituals
of a lost tradition, I pay homage.

A MOURNER

I put my head on my arms on my desk
to weep, and the smell and heat of my breath
remind me of afternoons at school
when the teacher made us stop our noise
and running around, and take a rest.

Not since then, except in love's
embrace, have the damp intensities
of my own body and feelings so
combined. My pain is this particular
odour, this primeval climate.

The teacher talked about an endless
age of fire and flood and earthquake,
everything changing, life-forms dying
and being born. In all the confusion
and turmoil, there should be a mourner.

LARK

Lark, lift my pain
above the rolling tide
and restless grey sea,
the yellow poppies blowing
on the dunes, into
the bright stormy clouds,
the sky's darkening blue cone.

Lark, ease my heart
as you soar and disappear
on a beaded thread of sound.
Let each pulse and throb
become a purer note
on the stave of your song:
music which forgets its source.

UNTIL YOU READ IT

Like music on the page
which has to be played
and heard, even if
only by one person,
this word, this phrase,
this poem, does not exist
until you read it.

II

THIS TIME OF YEAR

Parked cars on the street have pale leaves
plaqued to their roofs and windscreens
after the storm, and the same sodden
mosaic is pressed into the pavement
(the pattern fallen cloth-scraps mark
on a tailor's floor). This time of year
the last leaves on the trees are stained
with the watered colours of Mother's chiffon,
crêpe and sharkskin pre-war frocks.

This time of year, my mnemonic
for the date of Daddy's birthday was:
If the eleventh is Armistice Day,
it's the seventh; an association
hard to detach from such concepts as Father,
and God and birth and death et cetera,
when my father had gone to the war.
Nightly, in the double bed,
Mother and I read *Mother India*
together, enthralled by the gory details,
and tried to imagine him there.

They always happened in November
(several consecutive Novembers –
he must have come home then – Mother's
mouth would soften in remembrance):
our worst battles. To break his hold
and her power. There was much
damage. A normal adolescence.
This time of year, between the dates
of their deaths, with a swirl of brittle leaves,
foggy muslin veils and ice-blue glitter
(does it come too late, that promise?)
the forgotten returns. As if
for some purpose. Stronger than ever.

THE COPTIC WEDDING

Decades go by, yet I keep mouthing
the same stupid lines.
I notice a bird in the park and can't
remember its name,
but wonder again, for the umpteenth time.

Young women behave
as if they have been taught to believe
a show of ignorance
charms every admirer. From someone
my age, that's tedious.

Where lay the harm
in my mother's reiterations
and nervous denials,
except to herself? My impatience
when she insisted
she'd never been there, heard of or done it –
whatever was mentioned –
like a child who always gets blamed,
still makes me ashamed.
She seemed afraid of everything.

Being stupid – or becoming like her –
was my worst fear
as a girl. When I forget, now,
what something's called,
it can conjure her up from the ground.

Celebration noise,
ululation and the throb of drumming
across the formal paths
and flowerbeds, drew every Sunday-
morning stroller
toward its source: a Coptic wedding,
a dancing circle
of white-robed men and henna-footed girls
around a couple
with solemn faces topped by golden crowns.

Our hunger for ceremony matched;
side by side we watched.
Neither of us would rest until
old promises were kept,
neglected rituals performed.

Far from her own ancestors
was how she must have felt, uprooted
as that groom and bride.
Recognising a chaffinch, I knew it.
All of us spun out of orbit.

LINEAGE

When my eyes were sore or tired or itched,
clenching her hand in a loose fist,
my mother would rub her wedding ring,
carefully, along the closed lids,
sure the touch of gold was curative.

She also believed in hot water
with lemon, first thing in the morning
and, at any time of day, drank awful-
tasting infusions and pot-liquors
to purify her blood. She warmed
a spoonful of sweet almond oil to pour
into my aching ear, wrapped torn
old woollen vests around my throat,
and blistered my chest with a poultice
if I came down with a cold.

Remedies and simples from the old
country, still useful in the city,
were passed from mother to daughter
and not yet scorned. We rarely saw
a doctor. When I was little
it seemed normal to be sickly
for half of the year. I never told her
that I was proud she was a witch.

CHOOSING

How I yearned for a velvet dress
with a shirred waist and lace collar
like all my friends, but couldn't choose
which colour – dull green or
lurid red. It seemed a contest
between the nursery horrors
of a fairy-story forest
and the scary glamour
of portentous tomorrows – crazy
guesses and conjurations based on
grown-ups' talk, books and movies.

There is a photo of me
in a garment almost the pattern
of that ideal model.
Above the collar, a self-conscious
face, tormented by the problem
of choice – and every other
(which from the vantage of the present
moment, still make me want
to laugh or weep or fight).
So was it red, green or blue
I chose? I – or my mother.

NAILS AND SPIDERS AND JACKS

First, four flat-headed shiny tacks
had to be hammered into the top
of an empty wooden spool, after
the last span of thread was unreeled, measured
the full stretch of my mother's arm,
and pushed through the eye of a needle.
Then I'd untangle ends of crochet
skeins and darning wool from her workbox
and take one of her crimped and coppery
hairpins – which was just the right tool
for looping yarn up and over the tacks
and through the bobbin's hollow centre.
As long as I went on making the same
movements (like a spider extruding silk
from her web) the motley cord kept growing.
Later, I'd coil it into a doily
or a tea-cosy – something I thought
was pretty – to give her for a present.

And there was a game we played: jacks,
with small glittery silver objects –
each like six nails joined together
in a three-dimensional Greek cross,
a dice-chassis, a tank-trap,
or a nervous spider signalling
his mating intentions – that had to be tossed
in the air from the back of the hand and land
on your open palm while trying to catch
a rubber ball before it stopped bouncing.
I almost choked from the excitement.

The jack's six arms had clubbed tips
like the four nails in the wooden bobbin.
Remembering one brings back the other –
a connection that seems more important
than the shape of nails and jacks. Perhaps
it was a diagram of how
a message travelled from deep in the brain
through fibres finer than gossamer silk
until it reached my body's furthest limits.
Those childhood speculations.

Crosses and nails. Sixes and fours.
Trap-door spiders and private pleasures.
The game can be played with stones, shards,
dibs or jacks. Checkstones were buried
in Roman tombs and Celtic barrows,
where primitive looms are also found.
Angels and devils gamble for your soul,
they say, with ball and knucklebones –
and not only if you're Christian.
But I didn't know any of this,
polishing my skill at jacks
or musing over my French knitting.
I might have been thinking, though, about space
and pattern and number, female spiders
eating their husbands, shiny metallic
broad-headed nails and blunt-tipped jacks.

THE X-RAY MACHINE

Ten years old, I loved to look through
the periscope of the x-ray machine
in the shoestore where, even the sunniest
day, neon flickered. Metal edges
and nylon carpets sparked with static.
Those sharp white lines I saw were tacks
someone had hammered into the soles
of laced-up winter oxfords or summer
sandals. Those chalky shapes, denser
than the blur of flesh (a popsicle
of sweet red water frozen around
a wooden stick) were bones, the structure
that held me up and would survive me.
It gratified, more than frightened
me, contemplating the future.

CLINGING IVY

Behind his glasses, Rudolf Valentino eyes
glanced proudly, slyly, timidly, toward
her smooth blonde hair and sharp profile.
He wasn't tall, but she was so much smaller,
it felt like having a child at his side.
Except for us, they seemed happy enough.
He called her his darling, his clinging ivy.

At the end of the garden path a tree was half
engulfed, dragged down at the same slant
his gaze took – and equally resistless –
by a hawser of hairy stems as brawny as a
stevedore's arm tattooed 'We'll never be parted'.
Last night's storm split it to the heart.
The view is wider, now I've dug it out.

TOSCA

Above the walnut cabinet where
Uncle Roscoe kept pistols and bullets,
moulds and targets and tins of pellets,
dust motes drifted through a shaft of sunlight
while my Aunt Ann and I listened
to *Tosca* broadcast from the Met.

I know it was summer, because a layer
of dust below the glittering swirl
dulled the linoleum's pattern, and that meant
the carpets had been stored until winter.

But which pattern was it, which room –
before or after our move –
am I remembering, where we sat
between the radio and the cabinet,
which sunny Saturday afternoon,
during the war, assembles
around me as I listen to *Tosca*
now, in a half-dismantled apartment
the day before a new departure?

I have heard *Tosca* so often,
I think I know each motif
by heart. The grand themes of my life
must have been already waiting
in the wings, incarnated as
the jealous woman artist,
Scarpia's potent menace. Those two
make the couple. Cavaradossi's
revolutionary fervour can
never deflect their trajectory
of mutual destruction.

Uncle Roscoe's guns and bullets
somehow stay connected to the story,
but he was gentle, indifferent
to the passions of the music –
and the wife he had chosen –
that thwarted fantasist of every
métier and alternative.

So much talent misdirected
into trimming hats and bottling fruit.
She taught me to listen to opera,
to believe I was an artist,
to read Baudelaire and to iron a shirt
as well as a Parisian laundress.

Tosca is telling the whole world
how she has lived only for art, and I
am in another place and apartment,
writing my notes, watching dust motes drift
in the sunlight, about to move on.

Aunt Ann's floral-patterned linoleum
on one or other living room floor
crumbled decades ago. Each house
was gone when I tried to find it,
the gardens asphalted over.
I never learned what happened to her
walnut cabinet, or Uncle Roscoe's
collection of guns, after they died.

III

BIRD AND WORM

The bird pulled at the worm for a while,
got it half out of its hole, then hopped off,
in that bright-eyed mindless way birds have.

The worm rested after its ordeal,
feeling perfectly safe. But the bird wheeled round,
to where it wriggled, confident.

The beak bobbed, only a few times,
but enough to drag the worm's full length
clear of the earth. Then gobble it down.

THE OLD DOG

The faint sound of a drill
somewhere down the street:
an old dog wheezing and snoring

under a kitchen table
scrubbed until its grain
stands proud as Braille

and the wood between
damp and soft and worn
as washday hands that grope beneath

toward the old dog's head
and twitching flanks,
to soothe him back into his dream.

THE FISH

Trying to think it through,
force my mind to hold one specific
thought, makes my brain convulse and twist in my
skull like a fish in a net, with a fish's vigour.

I see the fixed glare of its eye – blood,
jet and mica – feel the rasping touch
of fin and scale against my hand, the tail's
last spiny flick and panic-thrust as it
wrenches free; and I am left wondering
what it was I tried to think about, depleted

yet glad that now I can follow it through
                        all the way to the sea.

VISITATION

A foam-crimped wave clear and silent
as a sheet of glass slid across
the shingle that wets your feet before
you notice then dulls and vanishes

or a sigh of wind under the door
that lifts the carpet's corner a single
moment and lets it settle as if
nothing happened though you know it did.

REFLECTION

I write with my left hand, but
the one in the mirror
holds a pen between the fingers
of the hand on her right. Her smile
slants lop-sided, her hair is combed
the wrong way, she stands so badly –
all contrary, changed, reversed.

I want to see photographs
(my own face and its reflection –
unlike each other
as matter is from anti-matter)
close together, and contemplate
resemblances, opposites,
the person they mistake me for:
reversed and changed and all contrary.

PART OF THE CROWD

           – means not only
going with the current, but also
pushing against it: that almost
ecstatic fear.
           Above the surge
of bodies, anxious eyes
demand a confirmation.
Others, already surrendered
to the greater being a crowd is,
are vacant disks of light
on the flood's surface.

           And sometimes
it soothes me: drifting through
sale-crazed department-stores or
carried like cargo down escalators
at rush-hour, onto the platforms
of underground stations:
           part of the crowd.

PRIVACY ON LAKE OHRID

When I asked our guide
if this was the house
of a rich Turkish merchant
he said, 'No, it was built
by a Christian. Turks
had high walls and windows
facing inward.'

My friend laughed but
insisted, 'Your nature
is secretive,
a primitive
who fears a photograph
will steal her soul.'

She got it right.
I can't resist,
early evenings,
staring into
lighted windows –
though in my own room,
black reflecting glass
unnerves me. I always
close the curtains.

I imagine
a house facing inward,
a hidden courtyard
full of flowers
with a blue-tiled
fountain in the middle,
and birds that do not
want to leave,

where women watch
white clouds float and drift
between the roofs
through the mesh of their veils.

THE LAW

Like someone walking a tightrope
or trying to stay upright
on a heaving platform – first
one foot, then the other,
backward, forward, swaying,
arms stretched shoulder high.

Never before have feet
and fingers felt so alive,
reaching out to sense
the slightest shift in balance
and position, like the growing
tips of trees or vines.

For things to stay the same
they must keep changing.
So the way to change your life
is to be still and do
nothing, while everything else
follows the law of change.

TO WHOM IT PERTAINS
'To create, to God alone pertains.'
Sir John Davies, *Immortal Soul*

'Stop creating!' is said to a tiresome child
who's half-hysterical with tiredness
from survival tactics, waiting
for the boredom of childhood to end.

Or said to the girl who insists
there must be a meaning to actions and words
the other wants to ignore and dismiss.
She keeps worrying away at it.

So the child makes a drama involving
whoever, maybe the whole family
at a party or a public place
like a restaurant or a railway station.

And the girl leaves her hearer so weary
with the story that finally he agrees,
'Yes, yes, how right you are. That's exactly it.'
She contradicts herself and starts again.

Making something from nothing –
a definition of creation
generally alarming except
to the one (having fun) to whom it pertains.

THE PLASTIC BAG

If I imagine this plastic bag
(innocuous stripes of white and blue)
being blown along the pavement
exploding
as I step on it; imagine shrapnel
penetrating my flesh;
the primary black white and red
of metal, smoke, glass and blood;
am I easing into this dimension
what need never happen?

Some say: even to allow
such images to mushroom up,
as ink clouds water,
uncages only pain and terror.
Others think
that language can defuse danger.
There were nightmares
from which I woke gasping with relief,
disasters not yet suffered,
with nothing remembered.

The flimsy bag billows,
looking strangely full, packed
with all the grand categories,
endless problems,
disregarded warnings.
It skitters across the path
I can no more not follow
than the one who chose
the code-word for revelation
can stop before action.

THE PROBLEM

The problem of what to do
with radioactive waste
is not yet solved.

There are deep-sea canyons
off the continental shelf
where sealed cans are dumped,
mountain caves under the Alps,
Cyclopean bunkers
to store the glassy blocks
(their deceptive dullness
of quiescent magma
in a lunar crater)
fused and annealed
from the residue.

The problem of what to do
with this new being,
slick with scar-tissue,

this mutation, this survivor

50

of injury and alteration
by archaic pollutions,
pressures and forces
that gnaw into the marrow,
the cells' blueprint,
the soul's structure,

until fear of future
irreversible error
becomes the critical factor,

demands a solution.

iii

What to do and how to move
beyond this moment
which seems so final,
detoxify and heal
each molecule
of earth and air and water,
of soma and psyche,

how enact the decision
not to abandon the sinned-against,
the sin or the sinner
but exorcise and absolve,
bring back rhythm and pattern and order,
(how to love)

is the problem.

IV

NEW-BORN

From the roof of her under-reef den
a giant Pacific octopus –
whose suckered legs are meters long,
who changes tone when curious
from glowing white to glorious red –
hangs a hundred thousand eggs
clumped into strands, like clusters
of grapes painted on the ceiling
of Sennefer's tomb at Luxor.

'The rough surface of rock
makes the vine-tendrils and fruit
more realistic. The artist's
experiment has succeeded.'
the guidebook says. I remember
that tomb in the Valley of the Nobles
more clearly than the others.
An arbour of freshness and coolness
lay below its dusty entrance –
a foretaste of the Western Kingdom.

Sennefer was Mayor of Thebes
and overseer of Amon's
temple garden, three and a half
millennia ago – yet
the vivid colours on the frescoes
and ceiling look newly painted,
the lotus held to his nostril
still fragrant, the grapes luscious.
His wife is young and beautiful.
She tenderly touches his leg
as they stand at the offering table
or sit together, pilgrims
on a boat to Abydos.

The third leg from the right
of a male octopus is modified
with a groove for mating.
When its tip is pushed into
the female's mantle cavity
a long tubular bag of sperm
slides down to find the oviduct.
An octopus is a solitary creature –
this rarely happens more than once.

For the next six months the female
stays in her den, stroking
the clusters of fertilised eggs
with gestures I want to interpret
as consciously gentle, even
maternal, shooting streams of water
from her siphon to keep them free
of fungus and oxygenated.
She will not eat again.

Wasted flesh skin
peeling like blistered paint
off a ransacked tomb's mildewed walls
or the weightless husks and residue
of grapes pressed dry
drifting like a grey ghost
trailing mummy bandages
across the ocean floor.
Now the eggs are hatched
her purpose is achieved
if two survive.

A hundred thousand octopus-
existences break through
the membrane web that sheaths them
and float out to the darkness
of the circling current
like souls departing for eternity
or new-born gods.

THE CRANES

Far and high overhead, the cranes
were hard to sight but could be heard
the valley's length. Then a plane appeared
to pass through them, and that showed them
clear against the racing clouds
and vapour trails in the mild noon sky.

Each bird marked another point
inside an ever-changing space
or on its surface – like the junction knots
in the mesh of a strong net, where
a huge, half-transparent, half-
imagined being, powered by
its own fierce jet and surging thrusts,
was streaming out glory pennants.

We saw new constellations forming
as patterns altered in all dimensions
and trapped the pale print of an almost
full equinoctial moon.
The cranes veered and banked, following
the river's thermals and currents.
We saw cherubim and seraphim
above the Rio Grande.

LATE LOW SUN

A late low sun
shone through each small new leaf on the vines.
Rows of gnarled brown stocks
pruned for decades to the same height,
and this year's shoots
tethered along the trellis wires,
sprouted new growth –
foliage translucent as lime jelly,
gaudy as stage jewellery

– as if a flock of butterflies
just emerged from their chrysalides
had landed on the vines and spread
tender, crumpled greeny wings
to harden and dry.

Late low sun,
a fluttering in the air. A double-
headed creature
settles on the stony terrace wall.
Pin-eyes fixed
in opposite directions, antennae
at full stretch
and thread-legs braced, two thin and downy bodies
almost hidden
by dark-veined wings that keep shuddering.

All at once,
still joined, they lift and veer, erratic, into
the branches
of the chestnut tree, whose ruffles of buds
and half-furled leaves,
where sunset's intensest purple rays
strike through,
are the exact colour and shape
to shelter ecstatics.

FLOWING STREAM

Shadows of leaves
on the pavement I'm laying
with stones from the garrigue
are drifting across it
like clear water in a shallow stream.

Shadows of chestnut
acacia and elder leaves
ripple like water in sunlight
over smooth pale stones
which might be a stream bed.

The movement of shadows
silhouettes of leaves
speckle the cobbles, the wave-worn
limestone slabs of unclassifiable
lichen-spotted shapes

and alter the pattern
by glittering refraction
as the water eddies
around fallen twigs and pebbles
on the sandy stream bed, on the paving

until I don't know
whether shadows or reflections
wind or stones or leaves
are the transparent water
in a flowing stream.

THUNDER

I am very good at chimpanzees' work:
shelling almonds, picking stones out of lentils,
scratching a smear of food off a sleeve or collar.
I find a satisfaction in repetition,
superstition, and know the myopic's refusal
to look above or beyond the horizon. Half
of my nature is simple as a medieval
peasant. The other isn't, and that's the problem.

It's harder to date the complex of discontents
shared by any metaphysical primate,
who soon learns that pain is surer than pleasure.
A stubbed toe hurts, and the soul asserts itself
by the same token. Such thoughts are as timeless
as wondering how the planets started spinning
and why one cannot live forever.
Elegies must be the oldest art form.

Thunder rolls from the northern hills, and the lamp
on my desk flickers. Once, it would have been
an omen, a god's voice or seven-league tread.
Now it's only a nuisance, or a warning
reminder of how easily the world could end.
There are days in the present when I imagine, far
in the future, someone brooding on first and last things,
keening the dead, and tending her garden.

BUDS

From late November until the solstice –
what used to seem the lowest notch
before the sky-ratchet nudged forward –
I have begun to notice, on vines
and shrubs and trees I'd thought were dead,
half-hidden below those few
stiff, discoloured leaves that cling
to dull twigs and dry branches, hundreds
of swelling, glossy new buds.

Such confidence and stubbornness
make one reconsider. Those old leaves
protect next season's growth.
The blackish trunks can still pump,
through months of winter, enough sap
for most buds (their scaly sheath,
their fragile freight of protoplasmic
leaf and pulpy, pleated petal)
to survive, hold on. Once
you know where to look, confirmation's
omnipresent: not a moment's
hiatus between death and life.

SOLSTICE

A door swings open
slow and heavy
on rusty hinges.

A wheel revolves
heavy, jolting
against the fulcrum
of its wooden axle.

A round winter moon
disentangles
from roofs and branches

to float above
snow-blanked fields
and rocky mountain peaks
weightless, easy

on the humming pivot
star-gleam flashing
of the new year solstice.

ON THE COAST ROAD
(north of Dubrovnik, 1989)

A mosaic of broken glass (halting the traffic)
strewn across the sun-dappled, heat-softened coast
road surface, fills a larger space than when
it was a windscreen; and the undamaged door
of a new bronze Mercedes makes the crumpled fenders
seem ancient and fragile, like a chariot unearthed.

Two men, with movements as rapid as dancers,
cut into the side of the car and manoeuvre
the pieces apart. Is that sound the whine
of an electric tool slicing through metal
or a faint scream from the trapped driver?
The blue plush bear lolling against a wheel
and the red pantalooned clown appear unhurt,
but there's no sign of a child whose toys they are.

A high terrace overlooks the corner
where the local car smashed into the tourist,
like a box at the theatre. The terrace is crowded
with people pressing against the railings to see
everything better. Their faces are concentrated
but calm, like angels watching the damned suffer.

VERONICA'S NAPKIN, or NICK'S LAMENT

Veronica was listening to the guitar music. Her loose
sweater and thick stockings were the same raspberry colour
as her unpainted lips whose puckering lines, incised by
constant shifts of mood, echoed their texture. Her smooth
bare neck and face were so white they made me think of
St. Veronica's napkin. I wondered if she was having her
period.

Outside the window, a pneumatic drill and the irregular
thump of a roadmending machine almost engulfed the
quieter passages. Each auditor leaned forward at the same
tense angle in an effort to filter out the jarring
distraction. Their eyes showed the alertness of people
waiting for a vital message in a half-familiar language.
The performers huddled over their instruments the better
to concentrate into themselves and the music. Veronica's
darkened eyes were glistening and wary. She yearned for
the summons into a larger reality, like the musicians, or
her namesake.

The evening before, we had eaten Sole Véronique. In the
shadowless light of the recital room, Veronica's flesh had
the same pale gloss as the creamy sauce or my starched
linen napkin – or the napkin Veronica had given Jesus to
wipe his face as he was prodded along the road to Calvary,
on which the image of his features has remained ever
since. The flat fish sheathed in its sauce might have been
the dim imprint of a face, and the pulpy globes of peeled
green grapes, cloudy crystallisations of pain.

If a napkin stained by sweat and blood were stretched
and framed it would be fit illustration of this lament for a
dead young man. The music did not develop, but presented
a sequence of statements about grief, memorialised from
different angles: an aural iconostasis of pietas and
lamentations, with pneumatic drill accompaniment.

ART

Straightening the pie by trimming the sides of a widening wedge.
I never could get it right. Always an overlap of crumbling pastry,
or a slice of apple, seductive, unbalanced the symmetry –
until the pie was half finished.

Smoothing the top of the hash
(onions fried soft and translucent, chopped-up meat from yesterday
and mashed potatoes) I pressed the fork to make a pattern of lines.
Between the tines, the mixture squeezed through. I levelled it down
again and hoped no-one would notice.

Alone in the kitchen, left-overs cooling under the neon,
the radio audience laughing next door, where my mother listened,
smoking or mending a stocking, neither hunger nor greed
could really explain why I was messing around with the food.

It was freedom, being at home, my good fortune, who and where
I was, an abundance never questioned, that let me use
the stuff of life and death in the same way a child will play
with water earth stones paint and words.

CHARDIN'S 'JAR OF APRICOTS'

The jar is half-full with the soft gleam
of dark gold apricots, and has a sheet
of parchment tied across the top.
Chardin painted it at the same age
we both are, noting the different
transparencies and thicknesses
of wine glass and jar – and the decorated
cup with a spoon inside, pieces of bread,
crumbs and a knife, the orange or lemon
and paper parcel on the wooden table
pushed against a soft taupe wall
in the oval frame. I look at it
for a long time and the painting opens
into another sort of time,
with its own depth and light and meaning,
like a childhood memory. No!
Make it go beyond the old story,
but keep the timelessness of the child's
first concept of eternity –
which might have come while staring through
the reflecting sides of a half full
jar of apricots on a kitchen table.

ARSHILE GORKY'S MOTHER

Her death determined his aesthetic:
colours as acid-raw as open
wounds, soft as an embroidered apron.
Shapes biomorphic, protean.

On tilting pavements, clockwork locusts
and dervishes with arms stretched wide,
tread out the blueprint of an emerging
image: opaque Armenian eyes.

Surviving every transformation,
the unity between those figures:
the pale calm woman and the boy,
face suffused with a lifetime's remembrance
of when that photograph was taken,
and his engrossing need to paint it.

TWELVE SIBYLS

SQUATTING AT THE WOMB'S MOUTH

Swaddled in feathers and cloth
a keen old face peers out through
what could be the entrance to a burrow
or a hanging nest

but she is not that sibyl, so shrunken, so ancient,
who pleaded for death

her gaze is too cool
with an abbess's shrewdness, an ambassador's
judgement, the tolerance
and wisdom of the Great Mother

squatting at the womb's mouth
giving birth to herself.

SIBYL HANDS

When she adjusts my back or moves my head
and says: 'Come on. Let go. Loosen your shoulders,'
in that calm and neutral tone,
I imagine whole parts of my body –
embers when a wind blows down the chimney
or the lit-up city
seen under a propeller – would pulse and glow
to every sensor of a thermal scanner
whose arcane colour language
of computer printout like cubist paintings
in shimmering blocks of orange green blue red
explicates the future,

as she can, by the touch of cool-skinned palms
and long articulated fingers, make
the vital forces flow out from the centre
with her sibyl hands.

FACTS ABOUT THE SIBYL

The total lack of charm Heraclitus stressed,
that she started to utter prophesies
the moment after her birth and drank bulls' blood,
are facts about the Sibyl I find of interest.

She put the Golden Age far in the future,
not the distant past, and was as hostile
to idolatry as a Hebrew. She refused Apollo
her virginity, and never wore perfume.

She said that when she died she would become
the face in the moon – go round and round like the moon –
released from her oracular ecstasy.
Only a sibyl can outstare the sun.

AFTER POSSESSION

She stands between the bird and silent crowd
with her vulture epaulettes and voodoo hairstyle,

with thick veined hands as stiff and cold as clay
that touch each other, unbelievingly,

and the closed smile of the survivor's perfect
knowledge, total recall. Like a stopped cyclone.

PROFILES

I saw three profiles: hers, the bird's,
(hawk-familiar perched on her shoulder)
and the image they faced. I heard
those words, echoed by a raucous croak,
emerging from her open mouth –
one part of a dialogue.

Her features mirrored each suave curve
of his, whose bronze and golden crown
was marked with the same plume pattern
as the wings that framed her head. Then
she turned away. Her eyes rolled inward
and the words stopped. The huge bird
clapped its pinions, shrieked, and chose.
I saw them deny the god.

HIS FACE

This place must seem a larger cage to my birds
than it does to me. The dark passage where
questioners wait on shallow benches and
the cavern roofed with arching rocks it leads to,
the hidden alcove and cool cistern, define
our territory. Only at night, sometimes,
when no-one will see, I go outside to watch
the birds' black shapes move against the sky
like a loom's shuttles weaving stars and clouds
closer, and read the text they trace, whose fine
calligraphy encodes tomorrow's answers.

Then, with a special sound between a moan
and whistle, I bring them down to settle.
I am cloaked and hooded. The touch of a beak
on my lips is cold as the serpent's tongue licking
my ears when I was a girl in Apollo's temple
and learned the language of birds. What they whisper
has a trickster's glamour, but their night-
patterns between the planets incarnate
the god. For one moment, before the first
beams of the dawn sun pierce that image,
my flock of wheeling birds becomes his face.

DREAMY

Since early this morning
the big blonde sibyl is dreaming
hunched over, clasping her knees,
like a girl at the edge of a field
staring into the tall grass
toward a distant line of trees,
remembering where she came from,
how the look and smell of everything
was different.

One of the temple birds
has settled on her back.
The dusty weight feels comforting.
She senses it is just as mournful
and dreamy as she. The bird
is brooding migration,
a river glinting direction,
hearing again the raucous cries of the flock.

They know they will not leave
this place. They both belong to the god
now, forever.

WEIGHTY

There is such rage in her tilted head and distorted mouth.
She'd thought of mythological births, from the brow or thigh,
not a wet gag of bristles and feathers stuck in her throat,
vomited out. Anomaly between giant and dwarf.

Like a shift in the structure of matter, that creature, small
enough to hang round her neck among the amulets and
other jewels, became weighty as the densest metal.
They sank down through the temple pavement and
                                        limestone strata,
rivers' sources and roots of islands, to a dark region
where she must serve and worship at his altar, forever.

Of the hundred mouths to the sibyl's cave, not one had gaped
wider than hers when Apollo's goad bit into her brain.
She had foreseen it all. But there is nothing that will change
the future. Not even this impotent fury, endless pain . . .

INWARD

Her eyes are staring inward
into a space as endless
as the distance from here to the mountains

she has forgotten. Between
those peaks and this high cave
lies the drowned valley floor where it happened –

whatever gave her the look
of a violated woman
or a bird that clings to a storm-struck mast

and made everything fade –
like being formed from clay and breathed
into life. Or a god's visitation.

WHAT GREATER GOD . . .

What greater god possessed her god
(they wrestled hard, like two screaming hawks
till they became one gross bird)

and made him change his sibyl
to a faulty copy of what she was
(shoulders hunched and hands too large

and that new expression,
threatening yet uncertain)?
– useless now for any purpose

but as the evidence and trophy
of his triumph over the other
and her unimportance to either.

ELEGANT SIBYL

Having become an expert at false tones
as the voices slide lower or higher than intended
out of control, having heard so many lies
seen so many faces altering crazily
trying to hide their real motives,
having pondered the fate of those who came to consult her
and how little difference any words make,
her gaze is now withdrawn and watchful as a diplomat's.
Her lips, though still full, meet firmly in a straight hard line.

But her feathered cloak and tall head-dress of glorious plumage
are so elegant, no-one can resist her.
The Emperor comes to hear her pronounce almost daily.
All the rich men's wives copy her style.

Alone at last, she strips off her regalia
lets the fine cloak drop to the floor
pushes strong fingers through the stubble of cropped hair
and climbs into the deep stone bath of water so cold
that even at the height of summer she shudders, and in winter
the effort of will the action demands
has become her greatest indulgence.

Only then is she able to think of the god and wait his pleasure.

THE EGG MOTHER

In the same soothing tone the god uses
before he mounts her, she whispers
secrets that the stars and trees have told her
against the bird's warm neck
then grips him firmly around feathery sides.

His strong wings raise them high above the coast
and follow the river's trail
glinting up the valley to its mountain
source. Brought on the backs
of their oracular birds to a rock-strewn field

below the summit-line, sibyls gather:
the Delphic and the Persian,
Cumaean, Erythraean, Tiburtine,
and those from even further –
sudden green oases, weed-fringed islands.

As if it were the Orphic World Egg,
a silver moon floats up
to signal her arrival, and all the women
turn to watch the bird
settle, and catch her first words and smiles.

Using the same tones their gods do,
gentling them into submission,
she strengthens her sisters for their stern duties.
She is the oldest now.
Her time has come to be the Egg Mother.